# The Reforma

## in

# Norfolk Parish Churches

*by*

**Susan Yaxley**

*with*

**Photographs by Nicolette Hallett**

**The Larks Press**

*First 1,000 copies printed and published at*
*The Larks Press*
*Ordnance Farm House, Guist Bottom, Dereham, Norfolk.*
*September, 1990*

*Photographs printed by Witley Press Ltd., Hunstanton.*
*Bound by F. Crowe & Sons Ltd., Norwich.*

ISBN 0 948400 12 9

#  Acts, Orders & Injunctions affecting  Parish Curches 1536-61

**1509** **Accession of Henry VIII**

**1536** Images and relics not to be made centres for pilgrimages

**1538** Images and votary lights to be removed from churches
No candles except before altar, sepulchre and rood
The Bible in English to be placed in every church
Pairsh Registers to be kept

**1539** Act of Six Articles

**1543** Act restricting Bible-reading by laymen

**1547** **Accession of Edward VI**
Injunctions of 1538 repeated — images, pictures etc. to be
removed without trace and church walls whited
Pulpit, poor-box and chest for registers to be provided
Sepulchre and rood lights no longer allowed
The Bible and 'Paraphrases' to be provided in English
Act for communion in both kinds
Dissolution of Chantries - end of endowments for obits

**1548** Wakes, church-ales and Plough Monday celebrations cease
Easter Sepulchre rites and use of holy water banned

**1549** First Edwardian Act of Uniformity - English Prayer Book
Act for the marriage of priests
Use of beads, palms and ashes forbidden

**1550** Act against Superstitious Books - Latin missals etc. burned
Order concerning the Altar - altars to be removed from the
east end of the church and communion tables used

**1552** Second Act of Uniformity - second Prayer Book
Rochet and surplice only to be used, not alb or cope
Seizure of surplus church goods by the government

**1553** **Accession of Mary**
First Act of Repeal — services and doctrine restored as at the last year of Henry VIII.
Holy days, festivals, processions and all 'honest ceremonies' revived. Altars and roods restored. English books burned. Married clergy deprived of their livings.

**1555** Second Act of Repeal — Papal authority restored.

**1558** **Accession of Elizabeth**

**1559** Elizabethan Act of Uniformity — English Prayer Book restored and Latin books destroyed. Altars removed and communion tables used again. Roods and rood lofts pulled down. Fines imposed for non-attendance at church.
Clergy allowed to marry with the bishop's approval.

# Introduction

———◆———

Visitors to country churches must always be grateful to find a small church guide to be purchased, and acknowledgements are certainly due to their authors, yet it must be confessed that this small book had its origin in a sense of irritation that such guides so often seemed to be misleading about the Reformation.

By bringing the events of the second quarter of the sixteenth century down to parish level and showing in detail how church-wardens and clergy met the challenge of a considerable flow of orders, injunctions and Acts of Parliament, it is hoped that this short account may help to make the apparent desecration of our churches more understandable, whether forgivable or not is for the reader to decide.

Though the roots of the Reformation lay deep in the medieval period and patterns of thought changed quite rapidly in the early years of the sixteenth century, yet the first physical alterations to the appearance of churches resulting from reform only occurred in the late 1530s. The combined leadership of Archbishop Cranmer and Thomas Cromwell resulted in sets of injunctions in 1536 and 1538 which ordered the removal from churches of all images and relics which might be the objects of pilgrimage, and of all lights except those before the main altar, the easter sepulchre and the rood. For the first time a copy of the Bible in English was to be kept in every church and the keeping of parish registers of baptisms, marriages and burials became compulsory.

Political changes in 1540 brought about the fall and execution of Thomas Cromwell and a temporary halt in church reform. Conservatism apparently ruled supreme during the last years of Henry VIII, though much quiet work on the liturgy was being done by Cranmer and his colleagues behind the scenes. On the death of the old king the Protestant majority in Edward VI's council proceeded with religious reforms at a great pace. In parish churches this resulted in a thorough purging of all remaining images and pictures whether in stone, plaster or glass, and the whitewashing of church walls. The removal of remaining votary lights accompanied the dissolution of the guilds and chantries which had in many cases paid for and tended them. Clergy were permitted to marry, and communion in both kinds was granted to the laity, two measures which, in different ways, helped to reduce the barriers between clergy and laymen. There followed the introduction of a full English liturgy in 1549, revised and rendered fully in accord with Protestant theology in 1552. The old Latin service books were ordered to be burnt.

The traditional appearance of churches, already drastically changed by removal of images, paintings and stained glass, was further violated by the pulling down of roods and rood lofts, altars and altar-pieces. Screens minus their saints might remain, but communion was to be administered from a new table set in the body of the church. The abandonment of many pre-Reformation practises, the burning of incense, the use of oils, the wearing of gorgeous copes and chasubles, made many church goods superfluous in the practical sense, and they were at this time either sold off to raise money for necessary parish expenses, or seized by the government to swell the coffers of the king.

The drastic changes of Edward's reign were carried out with speed and thoroughness, but their permanence depended upon the life of the young King Edward. His death in 1553 brought about a swift reversal of his policies and a rapid return to the ways of his father. Papal power was restored and the Catholic mass returned; chrismatory, senser and pix again found a place in church treasuries. Latin books re-appeared from their hiding-places and roods and altars were rebuilt. English Prayer Books and Bibles followed their Latin predecessors to the bonfire. But, just as the changes of Edward's reign depended upon the life of a tubercular boy, so those of 1553-8 depended upon that of the Catholic queen. Mary's death in 1558 brought to an end the link with Rome and the authorised celebration of the Catholic mass in the English church. The reformed practises of Edward's reign were restored almost in their entirety. Communion tables replaced altars, roods and images were pulled down, both bread and wine were again offered to the laity and the English Bibles and service books returned to all churches. A considerable latitude was allowed by Elizabeth and her bishops in individual practice, but according to the letter of the law and the canons of the church a revolution had been completed.

It will be evident from the pages that follow that the structural changes to parish churches were, for the most part, carried out by the leaders of the parish community, the parson and his church-wardens, employing local carpenters and masons. Whether willing or not they were forced to act as they did under threat of the extreme displeasure of the leaders of church and government and the more immediate practical punishments of the church courts. There were a few incidents of vandalism and bigotry: church windows were broken in Norwich, the roods at Bramerton and Rockland were pulled down by over-zealous Protestants and four men were accused of threatening to 'pluck the parson of Rokeland out of his clothes', but mostly the changes were peacefully accomplished. The story is less dramatic than is sometimes suggested in those church guides which speak of 'puritan zealots' and 'icon-oclastic fury', but perhaps it is a more poignant one following the struggles of humble parish officers to obey their masters, husband their scarce resources and keep their heads above water when the religious tide turned.

#  Fonts and Holy Water Stoups

## Fonts

Generally at the west end of the medieval nave, in full view as the worshipper entered the church through the main door, stood the font. In many churches it still stands there today, for the font in itself was not an object of controversy at the Reformation. Only the most extreme sect of the sixteenth century, the Anabaptists, rejected infant baptism.

Having survived the hazards of childbirth the pre-reformation infant was brought to church for baptism at the earliest possible opportunity lest death should intervene and carry the little soul away to the special area of limbo reserved for unbaptised children *(limbus infantium)*. The first Sunday or Holy day after the birth was recommended and to delay much beyond this might result in a summons for the parents to appear before the Archdeacon's court.

The first part of the old baptism service took place at the church door. The infant was marked with the sign of the cross, salt placed on the tongue with accompanying prayers and the devil adjured to depart. There was then a re-enactment of the scene at Eph-phatha told in St. Mark's gospel leading to Christ's words 'Suffer little children to come unto me and forbid them not.' These words, however, were spoken not in English but in Latin and would have been only dimly understood by the assembled parents and godparents. The godparents were told that they must in due course teach the child to say the Pater Noster, the Ave Maria and the Apostles' Creed.

The christening party then proceeded to the font which was duly blessed and the chrism (olive oil and balm) added to the holy water in the font. The tiny child, as yet unable to see, was then anointed with the 'oil of salvation' and heard his parents renounce

'Satan and all his works' on his behalf, and his godparents make their profession of faith. Further suffering was to follow — three-fold immersion in the font, first on one side, then the other, then face-down. The child, probably in full cry by this time, was then anointed with the chrism oil and clothed in a clean white robe (the chrisom) provided from the church vestry and to be returned when the mother came to be purified or 'churched'. The baby was then presented with a lighted candle or taper. This curious custom would have been extremely dangerous to all concerned had not the child been tightly swaddled. The delightful brass of Anne Asteley in Blickling church, dated 1512, shows her holding the twin babies who brought about her death in childbirth. Both are swaddled up to the neck and incapable of holding anything. One assumes that one of the godparents accepted the candle on the child's behalf, appropriately since the godparents were about to be charged with preserving the child from fire, water and all other dangers. The ceremony ended with the reading of two gospel lessons.

At the Reformation this lengthy ceremony was both shortened and stripped of any elements which could be regarded as superstitious. In the 1549 Prayer Book the exorcism of salt, the re-enactment of the scene at Ephphatha, the first signing with the cross and the anointing with oil were all omitted, and the hazardous candle was also dispensed with. In the second Prayer Book in 1552 the chrism oil and the chrisom robe were abandoned altogether, the ceremony being further shortened and simplified and allowed to take place at the font and not at the draughty church door. To dip the child once in the cold (and not always clean) water of the font was held to be sufficient and 'if the child be weak, it shall suffice to pour water upon it'. If the child survived, the godparents were to teach it the Lord's Prayer, the Ten Commandments and the Creed in English.

Both before and after the Reformation it was allowed that in cases of emergency, when a child seemed likely to die soon after birth, baptism might be administered in private houses by the minister or curate, or even in extremity the midwife. For this purpose it was advised that a bowl of clean water should always be made ready in the childbirth chamber. All that was then necessary was for the person performing the baptism to dip the child or pour water on him and say 'I baptise thee in the name of the Father, and of the Son and of the Holy Ghost. Amen.'

The font was also, before the Reformation, a receptacle for holy water and as such had to be kept under lock and key to prevent the theft of the water for purposes of witchcraft and conjuration. The font cover had therefore become an important part of the furniture, bestowed with much ornamentation. Norfolk has spectacular examples of elaborate covers at Salle and Elsing as well as two of the very rare standing canopies at Trunch and St. Peter Mancroft in Norwich. During Edward VI's reign holy water fell into disfavour as a source of much popular superstition, and the font cover with its line and pulley became superfluous. Evidence is scarce as to what happened to font covers during Edward's reign, but it seems likely that the more elaborate ones, especially those decorated with figures of saints, were removed. In Mary's reign the bishops insisted that there must be in every church 'a font to christen children with covering and lock and key', and amongst other expenditure at North Elmham designed to restore the church to its traditional pattern, we find 'To Fyncke for settynge in the pully over the founte viiijd', and 'payde for a line for the funte iijd.' What happened at Elizabeth's accession is obscure. Some form of covering for the font was desirable for purely practical purposes to keep out the droppings of birds and bats, so it may be that unless their imagery was blatantly idolatrous covers were allowed to remain. Covers again became fashionable in the time of Bishop Wren. Next to their expenditure on Laudian chancel rails in the Winfarthing Parish Book for 1636 are payments for restoring the irons and pullies of the font-cover.

How often the water in the font was changed must have depended upon the zeal of the local priest. In the Edwardian Prayer Books ministers were urged to change the water once a month, but it is difficult to believe that this was always done. When, in 1543, a young Yorkshireman was in trouble for calling the font a 'stinking tarn' he may have meant it literally as well as theologically. He said he 'had rather be christened in the running river than in the said tarn, standing stinking by half a year, for when God made the world he hallowed both water and land.'

None of the changes in the form of baptism introduced in Edward VI's reign made it necessary or desirable for the font itself to be damaged or changed. Unfortunately, however, many fonts were decorated either with the figures of saints or with carved representations of the seven sacraments of the medieval church. The new theology rejected the worship of saints and reduced the sacraments to two, baptism and holy communion, the only ones for which there was scriptural authority. Clergy and churchwardens were therefore ordered in 1538, and again with more force in 1547, to remove all images and pictures from their churches 'for avoiding that most detestable offence of idolatry'. In Edward VI's reign this order was given a very wide interpretation and clearly included figures carved upon the font. In many churches they were removed with the minimum force, the faces only being carefully chiselled out, whether reluctantly or with enthusiasm it is impossible to say. Some very old fonts have survived virtually intact. The Norman font at Burnham Deepdale is still in fine condition because its carvings of the work of the four seasons were entirely uncontroversial. Others have been quite badly defaced though it is not always possible to say whether the damage was done at the Reformation or during the early years of the Civil War when the Long Parliament (*not* Oliver Cromwell) ordered the removal of any remaining representations of the Trinity or other superstitious images.

## Holy Water Stoups

When, in 1554, the Marian bishops were in the thick of restoring parish churches to their pre-Reformation state, Bonner, Bishop of London, inquired of his clergy 'whether there be at the entry to the church or within the door of the same an holy-water stock or pot having in it holy water to sprinkle upon the enterer, to put him in remembrance both of the promise made at the time of his baptism, and of the shedding and sprinkling of Christ's blood upon the cross for his redemption; and also to put him in remembrance that as he washeth his body, so he should not forget to wash and cleanse his soul, and make it fair with virtuous and godly living: and finally to put him in remembrance that as water passeth and slideth away, so he shall not tarry and abide in this world, but pass and slide away as the water doth?'.

It seems unlikely that most simple worshippers went through this complicated thought process every time they sprinkled themselves with holy water, and it is probable that this explanation of the use of holy water was in fact a response to the criticism levelled at the practice by the reformers of Edward's reign. It does, however, give a clear picture of the regular use of the holy water stoup in earlier times. Sometimes a bowl or basin was built into the wall of the church porch or just inside the church door. Others were free-standing set on pillar-like bases in a similar position. A complete stoup survives at St. Nicholas church in Lynn and bases survive at Wolferton, Billingford, Blickling and other churches.

In large churches holy water was traditionally blessed before mass on a Sunday morning. The priest would exorcise then bless first the water then the salt, then cast the salt into the water in the form of a cross. Some of the water was poured into the stoup and

the rest reserved for processions and visitations of the sick. Sprinkling, especially in processions, was often done with a 'holy water
sprinkler' designed for the purpose.

The first shot in the war against holy water was fired by Archbishop Cranmer in his injunctions of 1547 when he warned the
layman against the superstitious practice of 'casting holy water
upon his bed'. In the following year the use of holy water was
banned by royal proclamation and the episcopal visitations of
1549 tried to root out a whole list of ancient practices including
holy water, holy beads, palms, ashes and hallowing of the font. As
a result holy water stoups were removed or blocked up. The
anonymous author of '*The Rites of Durham*' tells us that the Dean
of Durham's wife had two beautiful stoups of carved marble
moved into her kitchen where she used them for salting beef and
fish. Some clerical kitchens in Norfolk may have benefited by
similar acquisitions.

Swift removal back to the church would have been called for
in Mary's reign if the stoup could be retrieved, but at Swaffham
they had to buy a new one at a cost of 12s. For a while holy water
was sprinkled freely again, but at Elizabeth's accession in 1558 the
Edwardian rules returned and the new bishops, many of them
fresh from Calvin's Geneva or Zwinglian Zurich, insisted on the
thorough purging of popish practices. Holy water ceased to be
made.

Images and Murals

Looking at the austerely white-washed walls of most Norfolk churches today, it is difficult to believe that they were once profusely decorated with highly-coloured murals. Recent discoveries and careful conservation work have made it possible to imagine the effect of such decoration when it was new and the browns, reds, blues and greens were fresh from the artist's brush. The lives of the saints were the most popular themes, especially St. Christopher who was often painted, as in Paston church, giant-size on the north wall meeting the eye of the traveller as he entered the church, for, in the translated words of a medieval hymn, 'Whosoever shall behold the image of St. Christopher on that day shall not faint or fail'. Also popular were moralities such as the 'Three Living and Three Dead' at Wickhampton and the 'Sin of Gossip' which can be seen in faint outline at Colton church. Two gossiping women can be seen being egged on by mischievous devils.

Where there was an area of wall behind the rood this was usually painted with a 'doom', a depiction of the Last Judgment, but at Ludham there was instead a painting of the crucifixion put there in the fifteenth century, and the surviving remains suggest that there was something similar in this area at Cawston.

Statues of saints, some life-size, some much smaller, were similarly displayed about the church in niches, tabernacles and shrines and often standing on either side of the altar. The 'principal image', that of the patron saint, usually stood to the north of the altar and a statue of the Blessed Virgin to the south. The practice of having images in churches was not allowed in very early Christian worship, but it was nevertheless of very great antiquity. However, the stock of images in parish churches was continually being updated and by no means all the statues were old. Shipdham church, for example, installed new images of St. Margaret and St. Kathrinc as late as 1532.

Before many of these images of saints, whether murals or statues, lights were kept burning, paid for by the offerings or bequests of the faithful. The best candle-wax cost 4d per pound and this money was sometimes provided by small religious gilds which undertook the care of particular lights, and sometimes by money left in wills like that of Margaret Stannow, a widow of Aylsham who died in 1487 and left, amongst other bequests, '1 li of waxe to a candell, to be brente be forn the ymage of our lady in the chapell in the East ther.' Julian Stede of Litcham in 1507 actually left some of his hives of bees to the church to provide wax for 'a lyte afore the image of Sent Erasme, and another lyte afore the image of Sent Nicholas, and the iijd afore the ymage of the Crucifix on the Rode, and a Tapur afore the sepulcre at Estern, as long as it pleasyth God to kepe the seyd benne [bees]...'

The worship of saints and the making of pilgrimages to the shrines of saints were two of the earliest features of popular worship to be attacked by reformers such as Thomas Bilney. Amongst his reported sayings, recorded by John Foxe, were ,that Christen men ought to worship God only and no sayntes', 'that Christen people should set up no lightes before the images of saynts, for saynts in heaven need no light, and the images have no eyes to see', and 'our Saviour Christe is our mediator between us and the father: what should we need then to seeke any seynt for remedy?'

Bilney was convicted as a heretic by Bishop Nyxe of Norwich and burnt in the Lollards' Pit outside the walls of Norwich in 1531, but by 1536 many of his opinions had become acceptable to King Henry VIII and his ministers. Injunctions drawn up in that year by the King and his Vicar-General, Thomas Cromwell, forbade the clergy to 'set forth or extol any images, relics, or miracles for any superstition or lucre, nor allure the people by any enticements to the pilgrimage of any saint as though it were proper or peculiar to that saint to give this commodity or that...'. Two years later this was followed by an order that 'for avoiding that most detestable offence of idolatry' such images must be taken down, no lights or tapers were to be lit before any images of saints. Further light is shed on practices that were then common by Bishop Shaxton's instructions to his clergy in Salisbury diocese that they should 'suffer no night watches in your churches or chapels, neither decking of images with gold, silver, clothes, lights or herbs; nor the people to kneel to them, nor worship them, nor offer candles, oats, cake-bread, cheese, wool or any other such things', but they should teach their flocks merely to look upon such pictures 'as one looketh upon a book.'

How far these instructions were ever obeyed in the years between 1538 and the death of Henry VIII in 1547 is not at all clear. There was a conservative political reaction in 1540; Cromwell fell from favour and was swiftly executed. The Duke of Norfolk's faction became dominant until his son's activities brought him disgrace and imprisonment in 1546. Thomas Howard, third Duke of Norfolk, was a died-in-the-wool conservative, a man who boasted that he had never read the scriptures in English and who declared that 'life was merry in England afore the New Learning came in'. It seems unlikely that while his party ruled the roost the reforms of Cromwell and Cranmer were enforced.

Certainly when Edward VI became king his Protestant Council, which included Cranmer, felt it necessary to reissue the injunctions of 1538 with added strength, ordering that the clergy should 'take away, utterly extinct, and destroy' all shrines, candlesticks, pictures and 'all other monuments of feigned miracles, pilgrimages, idolatry and superstition.' It was at this time (1547-8) that most Norfolk parishes cleared their churches of images and white-washed their walls, completely covering up all the pictures so that they were 'utterly extinct'. Shipdham churchwardens' accounts for 1547 note the expenditure of 10d 'in expenses when we toke downe the images' and 2s. for 'puttyng out the images of the alter clothys' (though the method of doing this is not revealed).

Putting out the images was not very expensive. Whiting the church walls made much heavier demands on parish funds. Many churchwardens, who admitted later that they had sold items of church plate at this time, claimed to have spent part of the money raised on the 'whiting of the church'. In the Swaffham Town Book for the first year of Edward VI many intriguing details of the whiting process are revealed. 'Lawrensse the mason' was employed to do the work and two local men were provided to help him set up the ladders and fetch the lime. Size to bind the lime-wash was made by boiling up strips of cow-hide called 'gluwes speckes'. They had two pails of whiting, a bowl of mortar and a supply of hemp and 'naylle' to hold the wash firm. A painter was employed at the same time to paint the rood-loft white and when all was done it was found that many of the pews or 'stolyes' were bespattered with paint and lime, so one of the local men, Harry Bryan, had to be paid for a day's work cleaning them up. John Bruer had to be paid a shilling for storing the ladders and other gear and somehow or other one of the ladders got broken and had to be repaired at a further cost of 6d.

Finding the finished work somewhat stark and austere, those churches which could afford it were permitted to paint upon the walls selected extracts from the scriptures in English. Thus at St. Mary Coslany in Norwich they paid five marks 'to the paynter for wryting upon the walle in the church necessary scryptures'. The Ten Commandments were the most popular and useful text, for every child had to learn these before confirmation. The Lord's Prayer, the Creed and the Articles of Faith had also to be learnt, but are less frequently found on church walls.

Congregations had just five years in which to accustom themselves to their newly stripped and whitened churches. At Mary's accession there was a determined attempt to restore churches to their pre-Edwardian state but many wooden images would have been burnt and most murals were beyond reclaim. So great was the expense of buying Latin books and replacing church plate and rebuilding the rood that it was not until 1556 that Swaffham paid 'yonge Shortyng' for painting a new picture of St. Peter, their patron saint, and not until 1557 that Shipdham churchwardens paid 36s.4d for 'making the images of al hallowes & the paynting'. Meanwhile as a gesture to the new regime they 'painted out' the scriptures which had been put up in the previous reign. Swaffham churchwardens paid 'the paynter Shorten' for a day's work 'putten owte the scripture in the churche'. It would be interesting to know whether this was the same man who had painstakingly put them up just a few years before.

At Elizabeth's accession images and pictures were again removed and amongst Bishop Parkhurst's first set of orders to his clergy was one to stop up the holes where images had been. Scriptures, on the other hand, came back into favour and Ten Commandments boards at the east end of the church became compulsory, though the fact that there were presentments in the church courts for failing to provide these throughout the Elizabethan period shows that not even bishops were always obeyed. Fine examples of these boards survive in Norfolk at Great Snoring, Shipdham and Tivetshall.

# 🕮   Windows   🕮

Much of what has been said about the fate of wall paintings is also relevant to stained glass windows. Most churches by the early sixteenth century were fully glazed and many windows were of pictorial stained glass depicting a great variety of subjects, but with a strong bias towards hagiography.

Glass was fragile and at the mercy of misguided boys, birds and the weather. North Elmham's churchwardens in 1545 contracted with the local glazier, William Tylneye to take down and repair the clerestorey windows (presumably of white glass) for twenty shillings and thereafter 'he shall substancyally kepe ye seyd windowes of ye clerye storyes duryng hys lyffe naturall at his own xpse, coste & charge for xijd ye yere'. As the cost of repairing a single pane is elsewhere given as sixpence, this suggests that they expected an average breakage of two clerestorey windows per year. As clear glass would be less expensive to maintain and would also allow more light into the church, the change from stained glass to white, resulting from orders to remove images, may not have been entirely unwelcome on purely practical grounds. Certainly North Elmham was quick to begin removing its 'idolatrous' stained glass pictures and we find the priest, Sir John Elveriche, paying 6s. 8d in 1542 'towarde the makyng of ye iiij Mydle panes of the grett wyndow yn Seynt James Chapell wt whygt glasse'.

However, North Elmham was in advance of most parishes, stained glass being most commonly removed between 1547 and 1552. During these years many churchwardens sold off superfluous church plate, relics, tabernacles and vestments to pay for the necessary alterations in their churches. The government acted, somewhat belatedly, to prevent this and parishes which had sold any goods had to produce certificates to show that the sales had been with the consent of the parishioners and that the proceeds had been put to good and proper use. These certificates provide interesting detail of what happened to some of Norfolk's medieval stained glass.

At Weybourne they sold off church goods to the value of £11 12s. and, amongst other expenditure, paid 30s. for 'whything of the churche' and 40s. for 'defacyng of the glasse wyndowes'. At Bodham they managed to get both these jobs done for 20s. In Norwich churches the stained glass seems to have disappeared fairly quickly in many churches. At St. Michael at Plea the church-wardens laid out the great sum of £20 for 'the new glassing of xvij wyndows wherein were conteyned the lyves of certen proph-ane histories and other olde wyndows in our church'. Broken fragments from these windows, later reset into the east window, show that these 'prophane histories' probably included the story of Daniel and Belshazzar's feast, the Coronation of the Virgin and the Nine Orders of Angels.

At St. Mary Coslany they had fifteen windows re-glazed for £17, but the best bargain seems to have been obtained for St. George's Colegate where they paid £13 for 'glasynge of xxviij wyndows wyth whyght glasse, wych war glasyd with faynde storys'. At St. John Ber Street the subject of the stained glass is actually revealed by the entry in the certificate, 'for makyng of a glasse wyndow wherein Thomas Beckett was, xixs.'

The expenditure for this work was not inconsiderable and par-ishes could not be expected to take out stained glass if they had not the money to pay for re-glazing. So, undoubtedly, some med-ieval glass survived into Mary's reign and often very much longer. Windows depicting non-controversial subjects or heraldic devices would have been allowed to remain anyway, and William Har-rison, describing the England he knew in the 1570s, bears witness to the survival of many 'stories in glass windows … which, for want of sufficient store of new stuff, and by reason of extreme charge that should grow by the alteration of the same into white

2. Detail of the baptism panel the angel below holds a chrismatory.

1. Seven sacraments font and cover at Salle.

3. Painting of the life of St. Christopher at Hemblington, discovered in 1937.

4. Medieval glass pieces
in the porch windows
at Burnham Deepdale

panes throughout the realm, are not altogether abolished in most places at once, but by little and little suffered to decay, that white glass may be provided and set up in their rooms.'

When Mary reversed the changes of Edward VI's reign it does not seem to have been the practise to attempt to put back the stained glass. Presumably what had been broken was deemed past retrieving. Certainly such accounts as survive, whilst full of the restoration of other church furnishings necessary for the revived mass, have no references to payments to glaziers for putting back old glass. Pieces of old windows doubtless lay around in church-yards and other neglected places for many years and some of these have been retrieved in modern times, put together in haphazard fashion and set into modern windows as roundels like those in the south windows of Banningham church.

# Tabernacles and Shrines

Commemoration of the saints in medieval churches was achieved not only by paintings, images and glass pictures, but also by the construction of tabernacles and shrines which might contain genuine or supposed relics of the saints, their bones or their possessions.

Tabernacles were generally images hanging in frames suspended from the roof of the church; they were surrounded with canvas canopies sometimes of great height. A description of such a tabernacle can be found in Roger Martyn's record of Long Melford church in Suffolk written during the reign of Elizabeth. 'In the tabernacle at the South End [of the altar in the Jesus Aisle] there was a fair image of our Blessed Lady having the afflicted body of her dear Son, as he was taken down off the Cross lying along on her lap, the tears as it were running down pitifully upon her beautiful cheeks, as it seemed bedewing the said sweet body of her Son, and therefore named the Image of our Lady of Pity.' He also describes the tabernacle at the north end of the main altar as being 'a goodly tilt tabernacle reaching up to the roof of the chancel, in the which there was one large fair gilt image of the Holy Trinity.'

A number of small shrines also existed in Norfolk, based upon relics or statues, and some were centres of pilgrimage. The shrine of St. Walstan of Bawburgh and the holy well there had become so popular in the fifteenth century that a special chapel had been constructed at the north-west corner of the church. Wills of the early sixteenth century show that pious people were still leaving money to 'St. John's Head at Trimingham', the 'Sword of Winfarthing', 'St. Albert of Cringleford' and 'Our Lady of Pity at Horstead' — presumably a statue like the one described above at Melford.

Such shrines were some of the first physical items in churches to be attacked by the reformers, being obviously open to the charge that they encouraged idolatry and superstition amongst the uneducated laity. Bishop Shaxton of Salisbury wrote at the time that he had heard of 'stinking boots, mucky combs, ragged rochets, rotten girdles, pyld purses, great bullocks' horns, locks of hair and filthy rags, gobbetts of wood, under the name of parcels of the holy cross, and such pelfry beyond estimation...being commended unto the ignorant people under the name of holy relics.' All these shrines, images and relics were ordered to be removed in Thomas Cromwell's first set of injunctions in 1536, and again in 1547 in even stronger terms when priests were ordered to preach against 'wandering to pilgrimages, offering of money, candles or tapers to relics or images, or kissing or licking of the same ...'

There is very little evidence to show how quickly these orders were obeyed in Norfolk. At Elmham in 1543 they sold 'a pursse & ij Combs yt were Relyques in ye Chyrche' for the sum of 3s., but the relics may well have been removed from the church long before they were sold. Foxley was more dilatory and was in trouble with the church court in 1548 because there were tabernacles still hanging in the chancel.

Whether they went early or late, the destruction of relics, shrines and tabernacles seems to have been sufficiently thorough for there to have been no attempt at restoration in Mary's reign.

# 🕊 Easter Sepulchres 🕊

Many of the ceremonies which the reformers sought to abolish were of medieval date, comparatively late additions to the ritual of the church. By contrast the ceremonies connected with the Easter Sepulchre are thought to go back at least to the tenth century.

Naturally the ceremonial attached to the sepulchre rites varied greatly between the great cathedrals and small parish churches. The elaborate ritual described in '*The Rites of Durham*' would have been beyond the experience of most parish priests, but the essential elements were the same. On Maundy Thursday two special hosts were consecrated, one for the consumption of the priest at the Good Friday Mass, the other to be put in a pyx and placed in the sepulchre. On Good Friday, after the ceremony of Creeping to the Cross, a picture or image of Christ upon the cross was solemnly placed by the pyx in the sepulchre to the accompaniment of singing and burning of incense. At least one candle had to be kept burning before the sepulchre until Easter morning. This very special candle was sometimes provided by a person of rank, as at Hunstanton where in 1521 Sir Thomas Lestrange's accounts record 'Pd. for making & the waxe for Mrs. [master's] taper for ye sepulcre xijd.' The sepulchre, once occupied, had to be carefully watched through the nights of the Friday and Saturday. Shipdham churchwardens paid 7d. regularly during the early years of the sixteenth century for 'watching the sepulker', and by the 1530s the payment had risen to 8d. - surprising perhaps that this pious duty had to be paid for. During the period of watching, the sepulchre was draped with 'sepulchre cloths'. St. Andrew's, Norwich listed among its possessions in 1548 'a sepulchre cloth of redde tissewe' valued at 20s.

Early on the morning of Easter Day, in some churches, there

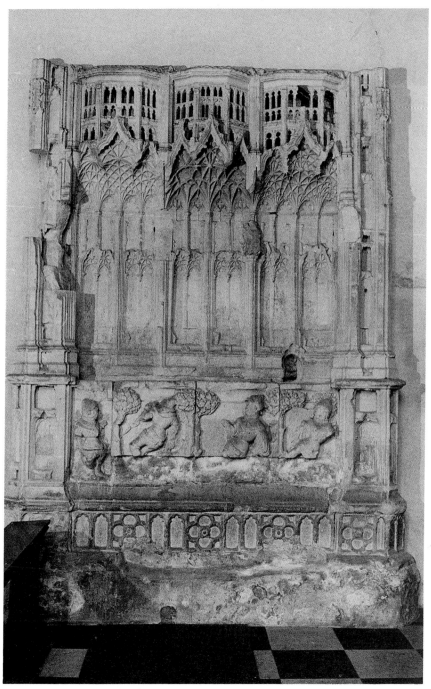

5. Easter Sepulchre at Northwold, carved out of chalk and badly damaged.

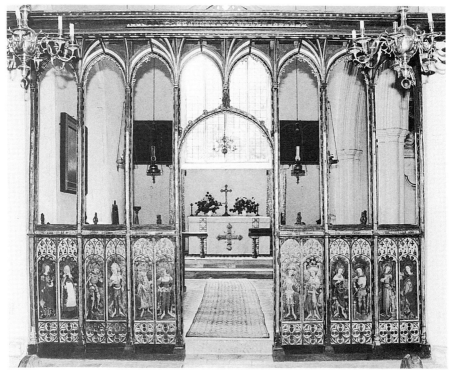

6. Fifteenth century screen at Barton Turf.

7. Detail of an Archangel and a Throne from Barton Turf.

8. Singing desk at Ranworth.

was a re-enactment of the scene in the Garden of Gethsemane when the two Marys (acted by male clergy with their heads draped) discovered the empty tomb. Finally the consecrated host, representing the risen Christ, was reverently removed from the sepulchre and placed in the pyx hanging before the altar while the hymn 'Christus Resurgens' was sung.

The proper position for the Easter Sepulchre was in or against the north wall of the chancel. Three types of sepulchre were known in pre-Reformation times; all were represented in Norfolk though there are examples of only two types surviving.

Probably the most common variety was a wooden structure, assembled each Easter and then taken down and stored in pieces until it should be needed again. At Shipdham they usually paid 4d. for settyng up of the sepulker & takyng downe thereof', but in 1534, woodworm or decay having set in, they laid out 13s. 4d. 'to the graver' for a new sepulchre plus 7s. 1d. for the timber and 2s. for carriage. Thereafter, until 1547 they reverted to paying for putting up and taking down only. One such sepulchre survives in a disused church at Cowthorpe in Yorkshire; it consists of a wooden chest with a heavily carved hipped roof supported about 3 feet above it, the whole object standing over 5 feet in height and about as long. Unfortunately no Norfolk example has survived.

There are, however, numerous examples of the second type of Easter Sepulchre, the permanent niche in the north wall of the chancel. Baconsthorpe has a small one, Kelling has one described by Pevsner as 'small but sumptuous', and Northwold has another elaborately carved out of local chalk. This is badly damaged, but there is no means of telling whether this damage was done at the Reformation or during the early years of the Civil War. The damaged figures are not saints or representations of the Trinity, so, on balance, disfigurement in 1643-4 seems more likely.

The third type of sepulchre can also be found in Norfolk. When a chest-tomb was placed in the north wall of the chancel, it frequently served as an Easter Sepulchre as well, a practical device which also pleased the descendants of the dead person, since the most holy rites of Easter would benefit the soul of the departed. A specific choice that this should be done was made by Lady Townshend who, in her will of 1499, asked to be buried at (East) Raynham, 'a new tomb to be made upon which tomb to be cunningly graven a sepulchre for Easter Day.' The tomb can still be seen, remarkable more for its heraldry than for its religious imagery.

Easter Sepulchre ceremonies seem to have continued without interruption in most churches until they were specifically banned in 1548, the adoration of the host within the sepulchre being too close to idolatry for the scruples of the reformers. Not all the bishops were in agreement, and the conservative Bishop Gardiner, only recently released from the Tower, was reprimanded in May 1548 for having kept an Easter Sepulchre at Winchester that Easter. Eventually the ceremonies ceased; the permanent sepulchres were stripped of their candles and draperies and left bare, the chest-tombs ceased to serve a double purpose and the wooden sepulchres were dismantled and sold. Bond in 'The Chancels of English Churches' quotes instances in Lincolnshire of such objects being given to the poor for firewood or made into bins or hen-coops.

For the five years of Mary's reign the sepulchre rites were revived. Shipdham's churchwardens, having sold off their old sepulchre and tabernacles for 30s. to one Gregorie Whyte in 1548, had to have a new one made in 1554, but only paid 11d. for the making and 2d. for nails. This presumably was a make-shift affair, for in 1557 they rashly laid out 35s. 2d. for 'making the sepulcre & for nayles, lime and pining in of the same' and in the next year a further 21s. for 'paynting ye sepulchre'. That very year Queen Mary died, the elaborate Catholic ritual was abandoned and the wardens were again burdened with a superfluous sepulchre.

The wooden Easter Sepulchre at Cowthorpe in Yorkshire

# Roods and Rood-screens

Roods and rood-screens were not a part of parish churches of the Norman period. Screens began to be erected in the late thirteenth and early fourteenth centuries, making a clear division beween the nave of the church and the most sacred area, the chancel, where at each mass it was believed that the bread and wine became the flesh and blood of Christ. Because it was necessary for the congregation to be able to see the host at its elevation by the priest before the altar, the screen must not be opaque, but able to be seen through — hence the employment of fine carved tracery in the upper half of most screens, which beautified and divided without cutting off the precious view of the host.

Above the screen and its loft stood the rood itself, a carved wooden figure of Christ upon the cross with figures of Mary and John on either side. Where there was an area of plastered wall behind these images it was generally painted with a representation of the Last Judgment.

The rood might be reached by means of the rood-loft, a narrow walkway which spanned the chancel arch. This was approached by a narrow stair usually built into the wall of the church. A complete rood stair can be seen at Wolferton church. Access to the rood was necessary for the draping and adorning of the images at important festivals. The North Elmham accounts mention the putting of 'silver shoes' upon the 'brown rood'. During Lent the figures were covered with a veil (generally called the 'voile' in Norfolk accounts), and in some cases this seems to have been operated by a system of cords and pulleys. In St. Peter Mancroft the roof-boss immediately to the west of the chancel arch still retains its original pulley wheels from such a mechanism. Candles also played their part in decoration of the rood — the accounts for Great Witchingham show that 24 candles burned along the rood loft for important festivals.

The extent to which the rood-loft was actually used during church services is still a matter for controversy. Pevsner generally refers to the lofts as 'singing lofts', implying that the choir was housed there. This may have been the case in large churches and cathedrals, but the narrowness of many country church rood-lofts makes them seem unlikely perches for bands of singers. It would be a rash priest who allowed mischievous choir-boys the freedom of the rood-loft. However, it does seem that at times the priest himself used the height of the loft to add drama to special occasions. At Long Melford in Suffolk, Roger Martyn remembered that in his youth 'on Good Friday, a Priest then standing by the Rood, sang the Passion.'

The total structure of painted screen, rood-loft and rood must have been the glory of many medieval parish churches, but the rood, the most important 'image' in the church, and the saints painted upon the screen soon became the concern of the reformers as possible objects of idolatry. The pictures of the saints, prohibited in 1538 and again in 1547, were mostly defaced, their faces scratched over with sharp implements. At Binham they were covered with white paint and black texts from Tyndale's translation of the Bible painted over the top. Now the paint is wearing away and some of the saints are beginning to show through.

Roods were banished, along with all other images, in 1547. Parishes which were slow to remove them ran the risk of having them removed by unauthorised zealots. Four such were in trouble at the Quarter Sessions in 1549 because they had said they 'would pluck the parson of Rockland out of his clothes and at Bramerton church they broke the glass windows and pulled down Rockland cross and Bramerton cross.'

There is a mysterious absence of specific references to the taking down of the rood in any of the churchwardens' accounts that survive for the period. It is true that very few parishes have a complete series of records through Edward's and Mary's reign, but both Tilney All Saints and North Elmham accounts appear to be complete for Edward's reign and neither contains any reference to the rood itself, though the Elmham records refer to the sale in 1548 of 'ye clothes yt henge before ye roode lofte wt other small steyned clothes & ye images ixs. ijd.' A reference at Tilney in 1548 to the receipt of 12s. from 'the vyker for the cepulker & for the cays of the orgaynes & for the bake of the roude lofthe' may tell us how the rood-loft was disposed of there, and Shipdham's expenses 'when we toke downe ye images' probably cover the rood and its images as well as the other figures in the church.

Whatever the accounts may say, the rood at Tilney was so completely destroyed that, in Mary's reign, when roods were again required, it had to be re-made from newly-cut timber. In 1555 they paid 8d. to Robert Whorell 'for a planke to make the Crose for the rode' and a further 6d. to Francis Hudson 'for a pece of oke to make the rode on'. The carving and painting cost 5s. more. The restored rood at Shipdham, meanwhile, was to cost nearly 28s. plus another 1s. 4d. for the nails and the 'setting up'. They had a church collection to help pay for it, but this only raised 3s. 6d. It was not until 1557 that they were able to replace the images of Mary and John. The timing at Swaffham was similar; the rood was replaced and painted in 1555 at a similar cost to the one at Shipdham, and in 1556 they also installed 'a line a swelve [swivel] & a staaple to hang and drawe uppe wt the voyle clothe before ye Rood on palme Sonday'. The Mary and John were re-made from new timber in 1557. They can scarcely have completed the work when Queen Mary died bringing in the new régime of Protestant bishops who would order them to take them down again.

Screens as such were not forbidden by the Elizabethan church leaders, but roods and rood-lofts had to be removed. Some conservative parishes hung on to theirs as long as they could — St. Gregory's in Norwich kept a rood-loft until 1573 — but in most

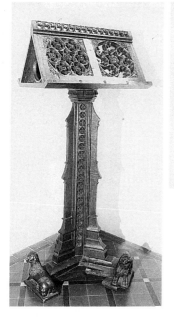

**9. Sixteenth century lectern at Shipdham.**

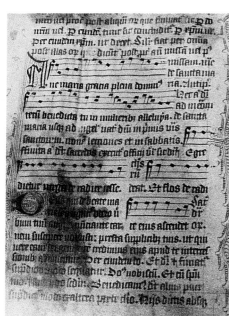

**10. Latin breviary at Salle.**

11. A puzzling arrangement at Tunstead - the rood loft now blocks the upper entrance to the rood stair.

12. Pulpit dated 1450 at Burnham Norton - St. Jerome facing.

cases where the 'pullyng down of the rode-lofte' was recorded it was done during the year 1559-60.

Visiting Norfolk churches it is obvious that many screens, parts of screens and their saintly figures have survived. The splendid examples at Ranworth and Barton Turf are well known. The screen at North Elmham also has a fine collection of saints which survived because the screen panels were thriftily used face-down to make floors for some of the pews. They were re-discovered in this century and replaced in their original position. The interesting little screen at Foxley exemplifies the varying fates of saints on Norfolk screens. On the side panels the painted saints have been altogether removed. On the left-hand panel of the door to the chancel are the two Latin fathers, St. Augustine and St. Gregory with their faces scratched out. On the panels of the right-hand door are the unspoiled figures of St. Jerome and St. Ambrose.

## 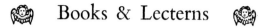 Books & Lecterns

The fully-equipped medieval priest needed a considerable library of service books: a missal for the mass, a breviary (containing an antiphoner) for the divine office, a manual for the priest's own services of baptism, marriage and burial, a processional for the prayers and psalms used in processions, a gradual for the sung parts of the mass and an ordinal or pye to set out for him the correct rubric when festivals clashed. Some precious survivals from these libraries can be seen in churches about the county, notably the antiphoner at Ranworth and the breviary at Salle.

These manuscript volumes were much used and needed repair from time to time. Entries in the Shipdham churchwardens' accounts for 1526 show expenditure on parchment, glue, '1 schepe skyn ... a doo skyn ... and iiij red skyns', as well as buckles and pins for the books.

The first addition to the priest's library in the sixteenth century was the Great Bible in English. Some Norfolk men and women had already, during the late 1520s, tasted in private the pleasures of the New Testament in English, having purchased copies of Thomas Tyndale's translation. This book was banned and ordered to be publicly burnt by Henry VIII's government in 1526, but cheap copies were smuggled in from the continent through Lynn and Yarmouth. We hear of Robert Necton, brother of the Sheriff of Norwich, being offered 200 or 300 copies of the New Testament in English by a Dutchman at only 9d. each.

Banned though it was in the 1520s, there was a great deal of Tyndale's translation in the Bible which finally found its way into all parish churches. It was the work of two enthusiasts for the vernacular Bible, Thomas Cranmer and Thomas Cromwell, to make it acceptable to the King in the 1530s. Thus in 1538 the injunctions which ordered the removal of images also ordered

that every parish church should acquire 'one book of the whole
Bible of the largest volume in English, and the same set up in some
convenient place within the said church..whereas your parishioners
may most commodiously resort to the same and read it.' Such
deliberate encouragement to the laity to read the scriptures in their
own tongue was quite revolutionary and not without hazard. By
1543 the government had found that this practice led to the development of 'strange and contradictory doctrines', and it was
ordained by Parliament that noblemen, gentry and merchant
householders might read the Bible privately, noblewomen and
gentlewomen might read it to themselves, but not to others, and
that common women and all artificers and apprentices must not
read it at all. This sometimes led to people being presented in the
Archdeacons' courts as 'common readers of the Bible'.

Though ordered in 1538, there were delays in the publication
of the Great Bible and parishes were in the event allowed until
All Hallows 1541 to provide the book. The price at this date was
to be 12s. bound or 10s. unbound, though some parishes seem to
have obtained theirs more cheaply. Parishes that failed to comply
were liable to a fine of 40s. for every month that they were without the Bible. The cost of the new Bible was to be shared between priest and parish; thus we find in North Elmham's accounts
for 1541, 'for a Byble for the townes parte iiijs.'

It seems possible that after the ban on its reading by the lower
classes the English Bible was removed from some churches. Certainly some parishes found it necessary to replace their first copy
in 1547 when its use in church services was first enforced. Elmham
bought another Bible, this time for 15s., and at Tilney All Saints
the parish 'paid for halfe the byble vijs. viijd.'

Another new book had also to be purchased at this time, '*The
Paraphrases of Erasmus*'. This was a volume of commentaries by the
great scholar Erasmus on the meaning of the New Testament,
originally published in Latin, but translated into English by the

unlikely pairing of Nicholas Udall, the playwright, and Princess Mary (later Queen Mary), showing that the work was revered by conservatives and reformers alike. The *'Paraphrases'* were ordered to be kept in parish churches for the edification of both clergy and laity. Considerately the churchwardens at Elmham laid out the sum of one penny to provide 'a matte for them that read upon the Byble and the paraphrases'.

New books required new lecterns. As the Vulgate Bible was still being used in services between 1541 and 1547, it held pride of place at the right-hand side of the altar and occupied the best lectern that the parish possessed. The new English Bible might well have to make do with something less elaborate. At Dereham, where they had a splendid eagle lectern for the Latin Bible, they paid the carpenter, John Outlaw, 20d. and 2d. for board in 1539 to make a 'lectorne for the byble'. Large churches had many more than one or two lecterns; at St. Andrew's, Norwich, in 1548 they paid 12s. for four new lecterns, possibly for music as well as bibles.

The legislation of Edward VI's reign continued to add new books to the church store. In 1549 the First Edwardian Prayer Book in English became the required text for all services. It was a comprehensive liturgy intended to simplify and unify the worship of the church; simplify because, as Cranmer wrote in his Preface, in the old days 'many times there was more business to fynd out what should be read, than to read it when it was found out'; unify because for the first time it established the same form of service (based on the Use of Sarum) for all parishes in the kingdom. Early editions of the Prayer Book had no music in them at all and had to be supplemented by psalters, but in 1550 John Merbecke's *'The Prayer Book Noted'* was published, the music being very simple and based on the old plainsong rhythms. One more new book served to complete the early Edwardian library, the *'Book of Homilies'*, ready-to-read sermons on moral topics such as pride, gluttony and lust, prepared for the use of clergy who were unable to preach through inadequate education or other disability.

These early changes took place under the Protectorate of the Duke of Somerset. At his fall from power in the autumn of 1549 there seems to have been a period of uncertainty when some parishes used the new Prayer Book and others quietly slipped back into their old ways, using again their Latin books. In fact the new power in the land, the Earl of Warwick, espoused the extreme reforming faction and gained for himself the description of 'thunderbolt and terror of the papists'. Accordingly, in 1550, an Act of Parliament was passed ordering that all the old service books should be clearly and utterly abolished, extinguished and forbidden for ever to be used or kept in this realm'. Any such books, and any remaining images in church or chapel were to be delivered to constables or churchwardens who in turn were to take them to the bishop or one of his officials so that they could be 'openly burnt or other ways defaced and destroyed'. The penalty for keeping such an article was 20s. for the first offence and £4 for the second. A third offence would warrant imprisonment. Thus the churchwardens of North Elmham, having dutifully bought their new Prayer Book and psalter, loaded up their old pies, processionals, manuals, graduals, missals and breviaries and took them to the Archdeacon's court at Litcham to be destroyed — 'leyd out at Lytcham for Mr vycare & other when we were commanded ther to Apere. And to bryng yn all ye bokes of ye olde servyce & for ye wryghting of ye Certyficat of them etc. xiijd.' Their counterparts at St. Andrew's, Norwich, had been quicker off the mark and had sold their 'quire books' to William Gilbert, a grocer, for twenty shillings before the Act was in force.

Wymondham records also refer to payment for 'the discharging of the church books in the spirituall court', but very few other records exist for this particular year in Norfolk. Swaffham, Shipdham and Great Witchingham all have mysterious gaps in their accounts during Edward's reign. However, it is obvious from the expenses incurred in Mary's reign that by no means all the old service books were turned over to the authorities. Many were spirited away into secret hiding-places and possibly used for private devotions according to the old rites. Some had been quite legitimately sold before the Act of 1550 was passed, others were rescued at the last minute, others still may have disappeared in various doubtful ways even after they had been handed over to the Bishop's officials, for the archdeacons and their underlings were some of the most conservative of the clergy, later spoken of by Bishop Parkhurst as 'popish lawyers or unlearned priests'.

The old books apparently disposed of, Warwick, now Duke of Northumberland, proceeded to the enforcement of an even more rigorously-reformed liturgy prepared by Archbishop Cranmer. The Second Edwardian Prayer Book was issued in April 1552, but the actual use of the new service was not to be enforced until All Saints Day. The Elmham accounts of 1552-3 record payment of 6s. for 'the booke of the new servys with the costs & chargs of hym that bought yt.' It was not to be long in use, however, for the young king soon fell sick and by January 1553 he was dead and Mary and the Catholic party were in power.

When Edward died, Mary's Parliament repealed his reforming legislation and restored public worship as it had been in the last years of Henry VIII. As quickly as possible parishes had to retrieve or replace all the old Catholic service books. Specifically the Act stated that each church must have a legend, an antiphoner, a grail (gradual), a psalter, an ordinal, a missal, a manual and a processional, all of which were to be found entirely 'on the cost of the parishioners'.

Out of their secret places came the old precious volumes, some to be given back to the church out of charity, others less generously to be sold back at a profit. Churchwardens scoured the countryside for Latin books. At Tylney All Saints the churchwardens recorded the names of three parishioners who were owed money for purchasing church books. At Shipdham, where church funds were well in credit as a result of sales of plate in Edward's reign, they quickly acquired two mass books, a manual, 'a wrytte processionale', an antiphoner and a grail for a total of 36s. 8d. Another small antiphoner was left to them in a will and the clerk bought an extra little grail for 5s. Diplomatically the accounts do not say from whom these books were obtained. Great Witchingham, by contrast, were still acquiring books in 1556 when they paid 3s. 4d. 'to Peter Shackle of Booton for a mass book'. At Swaffham they had finally to send someone up to London to purchase a (presumably new) grail and a legend at a total cost of 14s.

Whilst being ordered to obtain all the necessary Latin books, parishes were commanded also to give up their English service books. At North Elmham in 1556 William Rudde was paid 6d. 'for carynge the englyshe books to Norwyche'. Once again there were many opportunities for hiding away books in hope of future change; a corrupt official of the Archdeacon's court was in trouble in Elizabeth's reign for receiving English books from Yaxham in Mary's reign and re-selling them to Barnham Broome at a profit.

Mary's death in 1558 brought about another rapid change in the parish library; out went the Latin books and in came the English again. The Elizabethan Prayer Book was, in effect, the Second Edwardian Prayer Book with a few significant amendments, and at Shipdham they thought it quite sufficient to pay 12d. for 'mendyng the olde communyon boke', (no explanation being given as to how this escaped the bonfires of Mary's reign). At St. John Maddermarket they had to pay 5s. 4d. for a new one and at St. Margaret's, Norwich, they bought a new one, but not until 1563.

A new edition of the 'Homilies' and new English psalters were required in most churches, and during Elizabeth's reign other obligatory books were to be added, including Bishop John Jewel's 'Defence of the Apologie of the Churche of England', a comprehensive explanation and defence of the theological position of the new Church of England. Thus was established in every parish church a small library of books available for the education of clergy and laity alike.

# 🏵 Pulpits 🏵

Two types of clergyman excited the particular wrath of the early reformers. The first were the wealthy prelates who lived in ostentatious luxury and sinfulness, men like Cardinal Wolsey. The second were the most idle and ignorant parish priests who would mouth their way through the requisite masses, 'patter up their matins and mass mumbling up a certain number of words, nothing understood.' (Thomas Starkey, 'England in the Reign of King Henry VIII.) They taught little and never preached. More than once in Protestant propaganda such bad priests were compared to thieves because they robbed the laity of the word of God. 'Like thieves that were insatiate, they robbed soul and body without the fear of God's word, the light of our salvation'. (Peter Moore, 'Treatise of Things Abused')

The Reformation brought about a great increase in preaching and a uniformity in the provision of pulpits. Preachers like the great Hugh Latimer tried to convince the clergy that sermons should be a regular part of the diet of their parishioners, not an occasional feast, 'for the preaching of the word of God unto the people is called meat: scripture calleth it meat, not strawberries that come but once a year, and tarry not long.'

All large churches and many smaller ones would have been fitted with a pulpit by the early sixteenth century. It was generally wooden and octagonal in shape with no tester, the surviving example in Burnham Norton church being fairly typical. (The pulpit at South Burlingham is more splendid but less usual.) However, some small country churches were altogether unprovided and it was ordered in the injunctions of 1547, the first of Edward VI's reign, that the churchwardens should provide at the charge of the parish 'a comely and honest pulpit' for the preaching of God's word. From the evidence of the church inventories drawn up during Edward's reign twelve parishes claimed to have used part of the proceeds of their sales of church plate to provide a pulpit. It is not possible, of course, to say whether they were replacing an old pulpit or providing one where there was none before. The twelve include Weybourne and five City of Norwich churches where it would be surprising, though not impossible, for no pulpit to have existed previously.

When the first Archdeacon's visitation after the 1547 injunctions was carried out in 1548, eight parishes were presented for having no pulpit, mainly small churches like Warham Parva, Repps cum Bastwick and Foxley. The last had a practical problem in that the prime position for a pulpit was occupied by the gild chapel of St. Thomas a Becket - a small portion of wall painting from this is still visible.

Once provided with pulpits, parish priests were under continual pressure, during Edward's and Elizabeth's reigns, to see that they were used. Many ministers were not of sufficient learning to have received the Bishop's licence to preach themselves, but sermons were to be arranged at least four times a year and whenever possible two of those sermons should be given by a clergyman of proven learning, a dean, a master of a college or a prebendary. When there was no sermon the minister was to read one of the 'Homilies' to his congregation. These homilies make interesting reading even today, the language being strong and colourful and their purpose being chiefly to warn the people against such sins as idolatry, gluttony, pride, drunkenness, lechery and idleness, and to educate them in the essential Christian faith without too much contentious theology. Almsgiving, matrimony, even the cleaning of churches were thought suitable subjects for homilies, all liberally scattered with quotations from the English Bible. The government also served its own purposes by including a homily against wilful rebellion. Homilies were of varying lengths, some lasting less than half an hour, others much longer. The third part of the homily against the 'Perils of Idolatry' must have taken nearly an hour and a half if read in its entirety.

The provision of regular sermons necessitated a suitable arrangement of seating in the church. There are a number of references to moving the 'stooles' in churchwardens' accounts of this period, and it may be that in some churches this was the time when seating was moved from its earlier position against the walls to the present rows facing the pulpit, though the numerous surviving medieval pew-ends suggest that in many churches this had already been done. In the church of Tilney All Saints the rood and the pulpit seem to have been rather symbolically jostling for position, for the restoring of the rood in Mary's reign involved moving the pulpit. The churchwardens' accounts in 1555 record payments to Richard Alberd for helpyng the graver settyng upe the rode and removyng the pulpitt, xvijd. ob.', and 'for nalles to stey the pulpytt and the sayd crose, ijd.'

# Altars & Communion Tables

The earliest Christians are believed to have celebrated the Eucharist at wooden tables such as might be found in the houses of the period. The practise of celebrating upon the tombs of martyrs in the fifth century A.D. led, in the early sixth century, to an order for the general use of stone altars. Thereafter they became universal in all parts of the Christian world. The altar consisted of a stone slab over a chest, often containing holy relics, and it was marked with five crosses symbolising the five wounds of Christ. A fragment of such an altar can be seen at Great Dunham church with three of the crosses still visible.

In late medieval times two developments aroused the opposition of reformers to stone altars. The first was a proliferation of small altars, placed in side aisles for private masses and often dedicated to particular saints. They thus became associated with the cults of saints and their relics and all the dangers of idolatry.

The second development was an increasing emphasis on the sacrificial element in the mass. Although Protestant reformers held a wide range of opinions about the mass and the Real Presence therein, the position finally adopted in the Second Edwardian Prayer Book was that the Holy Communion was a commemoration of the Last Supper to be practised as nearly as possible as the early Christians did, at a wooden table with all those present partaking of both bread and wine. There could be no element of sacrifice in the celebration, for God had already made the one full, perfect and sufficient sacrifice in Christ's death upon the cross. The practical result of this was that stone altars had to be removed, no small undertaking in many churches where the altar was built into both the floor and the wall of the chancel.

It is possible to be fairly exact about the timing of the removal of altars from Norfolk churches. There was a shift in theological

13. Parish chest at Southacre with three keyholes for minister and wardens.

14. Sanctus bellcotes at Swaffham (left) and Necton.

15. Communion table at North Walsham – the inserted words 'and bloud' are just visible over the word 'body'.

opinion between the First Edwardian Prayer Book of 1549 which refers to the 'altar' and the Second Book in 1552 in which the 'Lord's table' replaces the word 'altar' at all points. However, the actual removal of the altars preceded the issuing of the Second Prayer Book, the vital year being 1550.

Old Bishop Rugg, beset by every kind of financial embarrassment, was persuaded to resign the bishopric of Norwich in December 1549. His successor, Thomas Thirlby, was not appointed until April 1550. During the vacancy Archbishop Cranmer exercised his right to carry out a visitation of the diocese, and by means of his visitors he ordered the removal of altars from all churches. The official order for removal was not endorsed by the council until November 1550, but by that time most Norfolk churchwardens had already done the job, paid the masons and carpenters and provided a 'ministering table'. The interesting example in North Walsham may have been one such table, since the carved text along the front uses the words of the First Edwardian Prayer Book and not those of the Second which had not then been issued. This table is something of an enigma because, although the Act granting communion in both kinds to the laity pre-dated the First Prayer Book, the words 'and bloud' were added to the table after it was made. Was this local people insisting upon advertising their rights or was it done on the orders of the Bishop?

A letter from the new Bishop to his archdeacons in December 1550 says that he knows that 'the mooste parte of all alters within this my diocesse be all redye taken downe by commandment of my lorde of Canterbury his graces visitors.' The surviving churchwardens' accounts for 1550 back up this evidence. At Tilney All Saints they had two altars to remove, the High altar and the altar of St. Edmund, and it took Humfrey Day three days to take them down. At Bunwell the mason and one of the churchwardens worked together for two days and the churchwardens claimed 8d. for meat drink and wages 'for helpyng to dyge downe ye alters'.

Later a woman called Rose Tyte was paid for taking 'ye stones that was of ye alters out of ye church'. At North Elmham the expenses of taking down the altars appear in the account book immediately after those for going to Fakenham 'to Aper before my lord of Canterburyes vysitors.' The work was considerable; the local builder, the churchwarden Herry Ruston and two other men were employed and a claim of 2d. was made for 'mendyng of a mattocke yt was broken'. The accounts also mention the 'takyng down of the backe of ye hye Alter and settyng up & tryming of yt in ye myds of ye quier'. According to another rather curious entry the painter William Tylney was paid 9d. for 'whyghtyng of ye sayd new Aulter & ye mynystryng Table ther- of' — whitewash everywhere, it seems, being the formula for theological purity. All these expenses were recouped the following year when they sold off 'ye olde Aulter, ye Sepulcre And s'ten other olde thyngs afor Acustomed to be occupyed in the Churche' for 8s. 6d.

The new communion tables were simple and sturdy and, for the most part made of oak. At Wymondham we learn that it was a 'joyned tabell wt turned posts' costing 2s. 4d. At St. Andrew's, Norwich, they laid out 5s. At Elmham they paid for a carpet cloth to cover the table though the only officially recognised cov- ering was 'a fair linen cloth'. The old sets of three altar cloths were sold or disposed of; many may have been sold earlier because they were embellished with pictures of saints. At Shipdham in 1547 they had gone to the length of trying to cover these up, paying 2s. for 'puttyng out ye Images of ye alter clothys'.

Scarcely was all this work completed when Edward died and Mary ordered the speedy restoration of stone altars of the tradi- tional pattern. The altars, so recently hacked out, had to be re- surrected. Many churches may, as an interim measure, have put the new communion table into the east end of the church where the old altar had been. So great were the demands on parish funds during the early years of Mary's reign that the restoration of altars seems not to have been given a high priority. Both Swaffham and Shipdham delayed the work until 1556, though both parishes had taken care to restore the pyx containing the reserved sacrament hanging before the altar two years earlier; Swaffham added to this 'a canabe or frame to garnysshe wt ye fornyture of ye sacrament'.

After the death of Queen Mary there was a short respite, a holding of the breath, while the new Queen, her bishops and Parliament hammered out the new settlement, but by 1559 the hapless churchwardens knew that they must brace themselves for further expenditure. At Shipdham they employed one Buckingham in 'pullyng down the awlters & for makyng the pavement ageyne ther' and at Swaffham the same man who had erected the altar in 1556 was employed to pull it down in 1559.

Though dogged by ill-health and hampered by an obstinately conservative team of archdeacons and church officials, the first Elizabethan Bishop of Norwich, John Parkhurst, was a determined Protestant and few churches avoided the new rules. The communion table came back into use, the only concession to the traditionalists being that it might now be kept in the east end, where the altar had stood, when not in use. In service time the table was to stand 'in the body of the churche or in the chauncell' and the minister was to stand at the north end of the table, not, as in pre-Reformation times, facing east with his back to the congregation.

#  Church Plate

The basic provision of plate for a church, if it was to perform all the pre-Reformation rites, consisted of a chalice (with cover or paten), a pyx to contain the reserved sacrament, a pair of cruets to hold the wine and water to be mixed for the mass, an incense-burner or censer, a ship to hold the incense and a chrismatory, a box with three compartments to hold the oils needed for unction, baptism and confirmation. There might, in addition be spare chalices, candlesticks of precious metal and possibly reliquaries of plate. These were the most treasured possessions as well as being, in wordly terms, the most valuable moveable items in the church. They might be of silver, silver gilt or parcel gilt, or even gold, and many had come to the church by way of pious legacies or charitable gift from families with centuries-old connections with the parish.

For churches to sell such treasures must have seemed a very drastic course of action, though it had been quite common for monastic houses to pawn their jewels and plate when financial problems were pressing. In defence of the churchwardens it must be said that times were hard, inflation and unemployment had done much to reduce their normal parish income, and the doctrines of the reformed church had made many items of church plate superfluous or, because of their imagery, actually offensive.

Some small sales of relics and plate seem to have begun during the period of Thomas Cromwell's ascendancy. At Elmham they disposed of some candlesticks in 1539, and in 1541-2, when they were undertaking great building works in St. James' chapel, they sold off 23s. worth of plate to Symond Newton of Norwich together with silver 'that was upon the Crosse yt the reliques wher yn'. At the same time a Mr Nycholls gave them 10s. for 'ye sylver shooes wyche wer upon ye brown rodes fete'.

Serious sales of plate, however, did not begin until after the death of Henry VIII in 1547. The reforms of 1547-52 rendered certain items superfluous: censers and ships for incense, the pyx for the reserved sacrament, the chrismatory, the cruets (wine being undiluted for the new communion) and a number of candlesticks. The new legislation also necessitated considerable expenditure on 'whiting' the church, replacing stained glass, and acquiring new books and music. Given this situation many churchwardens and parsons, in consultation with their parishioners, seem to have adopted a business-like attitude. What was superfluous must be sold and the money used for the most pressing parish needs. Plate was accordingly sold for the best market price obtainable, varying from 3s. to 5s. per ounce with the quality of the metal. Parishes may well have considered carefully the possibility that, if the value of their treasures was not realised for their own needs, their plate might well be swept away into the royal coffers for expenditure of other kinds from which their own people would feel little benefit.

In most cases sales of plate were intended to swell the general funds of the church, but in the case of Swaffham they had a specific purpose in mind. Permission was obtained from the ecclesiastical court to sell off certain popish vestments and vessels to raise the money to buy the lands of a chantry which was about to be dissolved by the Act of 1547, so that they could be let for the town's benefit. An attempt by four local men to get the land back into private ownership in Mary's reign was defeated.

Sales continued apace until the government became alarmed at the losses from church treasuries. A proclamation was issued to prevent any further sales and especially condemning any sales that had taken place without the 'assent and consent' of all the parishioners. Early in 1549 commissioners were appointed to supervise the making of full inventories of the plate, vestments and bells then existing in parish churches, together with certificates of all sales that had been made since the beginning of Edward's reign.

The inventories and certificates made at this time, some as early as 1547, but most dating from 1552, have been published in a number of volumes of '*Norfolk Archaeology*' and are a most fertile source of information about the changes taking place, the sales of plate and vestments and the use made of the capital raised in this way. The very full account of sales and expenditure provided at St. Andrew's, Norwich, is particularly interesting. It indicates a situation with a certain potential for corruption since the church-wardens were both salesmen and purchasers, but, if the account is truthful and accurate, these men paid the top market prices for all they bought. Several of them also made substantial gifts to the church at this time for glazing windows and putting up scriptures. Most of the plate and vestments were bought by Norwich alder-men, goldsmiths and wealthy merchants. What they did with their purchases is not disclosed, but most of the plate was probably melted down and remade into items for domestic use.

The spending of the money raised is most interesting and re-vealing. Modern churchwardens will not be surprised to learn that the most frequently mentioned item is 'church repairs'. The 'whiting of the church', replacing stained glass, and purchase of Bibles and Prayer Books also score very highly. Poor relief and road repairs are fequently mentioned. At Aylsham they sold off plate to the value of £102 13s. 4d. of which £40 was spent on 'reedifying the north yle of the church' and £12 on repairing the 'great brygge over the Kyngs ryver…which brigge is a common passage for horse & carte both to the market of Aylesham & to the coaste for the countrie.' They also repaired the school house and six alms houses described as 'very ruynous', The remainder was to be spent upon the poor of the town, 'fowre skore & mor which for debilitie of age, sycknes & extreme povertie are dryven to live upon the allmoys of the inhabitants of the said towne'.

Many parishes spent some of their money on the basic military equipment which each town and village had to provide for soldiers in time of war. When troops were levied for national armies each parish was expected to select and equip one or more soldiers according to population. With so many demands upon parish funds it is not surprising that parish armour, or 'harness', was frequently old-fashioned or out of repair, a joke in peace-time, but less amusing for the unfortunate soldier chosen to carry it into battle. The fact that so many parishes were buying in weapons and armour at this time is a reminder that during the years 1547-9 England was at war first with Scotland and then with France. The Elmham churchwarden, John Pars, was sent off to Aylsham fair to buy five daggers and five new swords. At various smaller places (Hunworth, Salthouse, Thornage and Whissonsett) they paid for sets of harness and for the 'setting forth of souldiers'. A further reminder that the county was on military alert is provided by the Weybourne certificate, dated 1547, in which they confessed that they had sold off plate, tabernacles and vestments to the value of £11 12s. They had spent some of the money on whiting the church, building a new pulpit, 'defacyng glasse wyndowes', mending the highway and providing a 'common hoche' (parish chest), but with the remaining sum they were 'determyned to make a gret Dycke and a Sluse to drown withall a sertyn marshe belonging to the said town joyning to the most dangerous place for ye enemyes to londe at in these partyes ... which they were commaunded to by my Lord Marques of Northehampton...'. Northampton, the Lord Lieutenant, had carried out an inspection of the coastal defences that year and other parishes nearby also contributed to the work which they referred to as the 'bulwarke' and also to the upkeep of the beacon at Weybourne.

Parishes which did not sell their plate lost out in every way. Local needs and causes did not benefit, nor were they permitted to keep their treasures for long. In 1552 instructions came from the Duke of Northumberland's government that superfluous plate still remaining in parish churches should be taken away for the King's use. Each small church was to be left with just one chalice and paten; larger churches might keep two. Considerable quantities of precious metal must have been cleared out of country churches and taken to London to be melted down. This seizure, labelled by some the 'Great Pillage', was still in progress when the Duke of Northumberland's fragile Protestant régime collapsed on the death of the young king in January 1553. Lady Jane Grey was proclaimed queen by the protestant faction, represented in Norfolk by the Duke of Northumberland's sons at King's Lynn, but support for Mary's more legitimate claim to the throne was pretty solid in Norfolk, and it was from Kenninghall that she proceeded to the capital to claim her inheritance.

At Mary's accession seizures of church goods were stopped and a few items returned, but it was too late to retrieve most of what had been taken. There was certainly no question of giving back the proceeds to parishes. The unfortunate priests and churchwardens were indeed told to replace the items taken as soon as possible 'at the charge of the parish'. The minimum requirements were stated to be a chalice, two cruets, an incenser (censer) and a ship for incense, a pyx, a chrismatory and candlesticks and two crosses, one for processions and one for the dead.

An immediate search began to recover items of plate that had been sold early in Edward's reign or hidden away from the commissioners at the end of the reign. Very few churchwardens' accounts survive for the years 1553 and 1554, so the process of replacing parish plate is veiled in secrecy, with just occasional glimpses of Great Witchingham retrieving a pair of censers from 'a butcher of Dawllynge' and Tilney All Saints paying a goldsmith 'for making a sylver pynne to the litell rownd pyxt to bere the sacrament'. Only Swaffham accounts have anywhere near a full record mentioning the purchase of a 'crosse of laten wt a staffe, a pyxe and a payer of sensers' for 42s. in 1554. A further payment of 5d. for 'the chrismatory mending and the pyxe' leaves a number of questions unanswered. Where did the chrismatory come from and how did it get damaged?

Even less evidence survives for the fate of pyxes, censers, chrismatories and cruets when these once again became superfluous at Elizabeth's accession. An entry in the Witchingham accounts reporting the sale 'by the consent of the township' of 12 oz. of plate 'for the reparation and amending of certain bridges within the township of Witchingham' may well be typical of similar disposals in other parishes.

As parishes gradually became accustomed to the rites of the Elizabethan church, some changes in church plate were found to be necessary. Now that the wine as well as the bread was received by all communicants the small medieval chalice left to them after Northumberland's confiscation was not really adequate. These 'massing cups' were in any case frowned upon because of their popish symbolism. Gradually they were replaced by larger cups. In Norfolk a very large number of chalices were replaced in 1567. Goldsmiths like Peter Peterson of Norwich must have been kept working at full stretch to provide parishes with goblets of suitable size and simplicity. This sudden zeal on the part of ministers and churchwardens almost certainly reflected pressure from officials of the Metropolitan Visitation of 1566 and from the Queen herself. Even so, not all parishes could afford to act immediately and Archbishop Parker was still inquiring in his Visitation articles of 1569 whether any clergy 'do minister in any profane cups, bowls, or dishes, or chalices heretofore used at Masse, or els in a decent communion cuppe provided and kept for the same purpose only'. Flagons, similar to those in domestic use, were also provided at this time to hold wine for refilling the communion cup.

A post-Reformation communion cup and a chalice
of early Tudor date.

# ✿ Bells ✿

Most Norfolk churches had between two and five bells hanging in their towers when the inventories of church goods were made in Edward VI's reign. A few small churches, Cantley for example, had only one; St. Andrew's in Norwich had seven.

At least one large bell and one small sanctus (saunce or sacring) bell was necessary for the normal running of a parish church before the Reformation. The large bell was rung to summon people to mass and to confession (the Pardon Bell) and also to mark the death of anyone in the parish (the Passing Bell) and before and after a burial service. The sanctus bell was rung at two crucial points in the mass, really as a means of concentrating the attention of the congregation upon the holiest moments, the saying by the priest of the 'Holy, holy, holy' ('sanctus' in Latin) and the elevation of the host. Remembering that congregations at this time included all but the most alienated elements in the parish plus their dogs, and that the audible telling of beads was almost universal, calling the people to attention may often have been a real necessity. The sanctus bell was often hung in a small bellcote on the roof of the church over the point where the chancel joined the nave, and was tolled by pulling a rope from inside the church. Sometimes it was hung inside the church and a surviving one of these may be seen in Scarning church, still hanging in its original wooden frame behind the rood screen. It is less than six inches across and makes a rather tinny sound justifying its popular name 'ting-tang'.

Bells in addition to these two were not essential, but were clearly the great pride of some parishes. Churchwardens' accounts, evidence regular expenditure on clappers, ropes and baldrics and re-casting of bells. When the parishioners of East Dereham found that their tower would no longer bear the weight of their bells. at the beginning of the sixteenth century they went to the great expense of building an entirely new tower or 'clocher' rather than live without the sound of their bells. Anyone wishing to reflect upon the unequal wealth of parishes should travel the few miles from Dereham to Woodrising where, the tower having fallen, they also re-housed their bells, but on a much humbler scale.

The great festival for bell-ringing was All Souls, when, either at Hallowmass (November 1st) or All Souls' Day (November 2nd) the church bells were rung all night in honour of the souls of the departed. The bell-ringers needed a good supply of ale to see them through the night and a collection was often made to pay for this, any surplus going into the church coffers. The North Elmham accounts for 1540 record the receipt of 4s. 3½d. 'att hallowmes drynkyng' and in 1542 5s. 6d 'for Halowmes nyght all thyngs dyscharged'.

Bells were also rung at times of public rejoicing, coronations, royal births and military victories and also when there was need to alert the people to an emergency, fire, flood or other disaster. They might also be used to raise men in rebellion as in 1549 when the indictment of Robert Kett claimed he had raised support by 'traitorous proclamations, hue and cry and the ringing of bells'.

Bells were frequently dedicated to saints; amongst the surviving pre-Reformation bells recorded by L'estrange in 1874 the most popular dedications were to the Blessed Virgin Mary, St. Peter, St. Paul, St. Gabriel and the Trinity. There were also many superstitions connected with the bells, as for example that the ringing of bells would prevent damage to the church tower from lightning. Thus on three counts, their connection with saint-worship, with prayers for the souls of the dead and with superstition, bells were somewhat out of favour with the reformers.

Nevertheless, when, in the 1540's, churchwardens began to sell off superfluous church goods to raise money for their parishes, they were in no hurry to dispose of their bells. Although a considerable quantity of plate was sold, very few bells went the same way. Dilham, Ingham and Wighton sold one bell each; Wighton claimed that their bell was broken, but it was the largest and most valuable. Some mystery is attached to events at Wymondham where a damaged and incomplete inventory survives for 1552 in which only two bells are declared and no sales of bells admitted. The churchwardens' accounts, however, show clearly that no less than six bells were sold in 1551. Possibly these were the bells of the Abbey, bought by the parish from the Crown in 1540, and technically not the bells of the parish church.

Events at Cley and Holt are also puzzling. The inventory of 1552 records, in addition to one bell in Cley steeple, 'iij belles weyng xxviij C di. delyered by the consente of the towne to the Lorde of Roteland'. The mystery deepens when we find that the Holt inventory shows that the Earl worked the same magic there, persuading them to surrender two more bells to him. Henry Manners, 2nd Earl of Rutland, was the son of Eleanor Paston, so had local connections. He was made Warden of the East and Middle Marches (of the Scottish borders) in 1549. It is frequently forgotten that during most of Edward's reign England was at war, first with Scotland and then with France. Could the Earl have persuaded the inhabitants of Cley and Holt that their bells were a necessary patriotic contribution to the wars?

There was another intriguing situation at Stiffkey in 1552 where the churchwardens declared that two of their bells were in the custody of Mr Calthorp but that Mr Banyard had the clappers.

The commissioners for church goods appointed in 1552 were instructed to reserve to each parish one chalice (two for larger parishes) and their smallest steeple bell, and it seems to have been the intention of the government to remove the rest for melting down, the proceeds to help solve the financial problems of Northumberland's government. (Bell-metal was valued at 15s. per cwt.) However, immediate instructions were to leave the bells in situ for the present and to bring away only the plate and vestments.

The accounts confirm that this is what was done at Elmham — 'for our costs & other Comanded to bryng ye Chyrche Goods wt yer Inventorye of ye same, Bells & a payer of chalyce onlye excepted...'. L'estrange even suggests that it was never intended to confiscate the bells, only to bring a halt to their sale by churchwardens. In any case the large number of surviving bells (250 or 1 in 6 when L'estrange was writing) is fairly conclusive evidence that no confiscation ever took place.

Protestant opinion was hostile to certain aspects of bell-ringing, especially to elaborate ringing at funerals and the all-night session of ringing (and drinking) at All Souls. The first truly Protestant bishop of Norwich, John Parkhurst, in his first set of injunctions to his clergy in 1561, ordered them to see that their clerks 'if they do ring at the burial of the deade, noone or curphewe, they ring but one peall, and that verie short, omitting all other unnecessarie ringings'. In 1571 we find him chasing up his Chancellor to take action against the ringers of St. Faith's, Sprowston and Worstead for unnecessary ringing of bells.

All in all, the Reformation did little harm to Norfolk's old church bells. It is one of the ironies of history that the revival of change-ringing in the eighteenth and early nineteenth centuries may have done more damage to old bells, for then a number of parishes, St. Gregory's Norwich in 1818 for example, re-cast small peals of heavy, ancient bells into larger peals of light bells.

# Vestments

The glittering array of ecclesiastical robes to be found in Norfolk churches before the Reformation may be studied in detail in the inventories of church goods drawn up during Edward VI's reign, dating mainly from 1552.

For the main church festivals there were copes of velvet, satin or damask decorated with a surprising variety of devices, moons and stars, leopards and dolphins, lillypots, flowers of gold, and a variety of saints. At Felmingham, for example, they had three copes of crimson, green and purple velvet, and at Littlt Walsingham they had a splendid wardrobe of seven copes, two of 'whyte caffa braunched with lillypottes', two of 'whyte damaske braunched with flower de luces', two of 'red bryges [Bruges] saten braunched', and one of white 'bryges saten braunched with lillyes & roses'.

Chasubles, tunicles and albs for the clergy made up the bulk of the remaining wardrobe plus surplices for the use of choristers and other assisting laymen. Not all these garments were in prime condition. (At Swaftham in 1536 they thriftily converted two old copes into one new one.) They had to withstand the dangers of storage in damp churches and of regular use in processions through muddy or dusty streets and churchyards. (A fifteenth century chasuble may be seen under glass in Burnham Deepdale church, but it is Rhenish, not English.)

The most extreme reformers of the mid-sixteenth century held that vestments were without scriptural authority and that, whilst the minister should be dressed with dignity and sobriety, he should not in any other way be distinguished from laymen. Splendid vestments were associated with an over-powerful and wealthy church, exaggerated worldly splendour and popish processions, all quite out of keeping with the reformers' emphasis on the minister's role as a humble teacher and pastor of his flock. Many moderates were not so extreme as to wish to abolish vestments altogether, but some simplification seemed inevitable when the reformers gained dominance in the Council of the new King Edward VI in 1547.

In the Prayer Book of 1549 vestments, that is rochet, alb and cope or chasuble, were retained for bishops, but the parish clergy were reduced to the severe simplicity of the surplice. Fierce controversy followed and by 1552 even the alb and cope were abandoned and only the rochet was allowed to distinguish the bishops from the lesser clergy. Extensive sales of vestments took place between 1548 and 1553. In Norwich they were bought by the aldermen and wealthy merchants of the City; they paid good prices for them and may well have considered that they were making a public-spirited contribution to the welfare of their parishes. When Mary's reign brought a revival of the use of vestments it would perhaps be uncharitable to enquire whether these gentlemen gave or sold their purchases back to the church.

With the revival of the Catholic mass in Mary's reign, vestments returned in full splendour. Bishop Bonner's orders to the clergy of the London diocese in 1553 stated that each church should have a complete suit of vestments for principal feasts, vestments for deacon and sub-deacon, a cope with all its appurtenances (amice, alb, girdle, stole and fannon), three surplices and a rochet. Clergy were also required to change their appearance in other ways. The reforming ministers had not only taken advantage of the Edwardian legislation permitting them to marry, they had also abandoned the medieval tonsure and allowed both hair and beard to grow, thus assuming both the life-pattern and the appearance of laymen. Mary peremptorily ordered them to shave off their beards and tonsure their heads.

It is not possible to say how many of the vestments which were disposed of in Edward's reign were able to be retrieved in Mary's time. Many may already have been converted to domestic hangings or clothing, or perhaps have taken pride of place in the private chapels of those who clung to the old ways. What happened, one wonders, to the 'cope of cloth a tyssue' which Wymondham had delivered into the hands of Sir John Robsart in Edward's reign and remained 'unprised' and to the 'vestment of black vellet' similarly in the hands of Lady Knyvett?

Out on display again during Mary's reign, vestments were to disappear from parish churches once more when Elizabeth came to the throne. Copes, albs and chasubles were retained for use in cathedrals, but the humble parish parson was to clothe his cassock only in a surplice, elevated from its role as a medieval chorister's robe to become the distinctive dress of the Elizabethan clergy. Even this simple garment remained a bone of contention with the more puritanical clergy who found frequent excuses for not wearing it, but, from a practical viewpoint, it had the advantage of being washable and easily repaired or replaced.

The sixteenth century church thus lost a large proportion of its wardrobe of vestments, rich in material, embroidery and symbolism, but not all disappeared entirely without trace. The parish players of Bungay in 1577 were to be seen arrayed in 'gownes & coats that were made of certayne pec's of olld copes', and some enterprising dealers appear to have made a profit out of shipping 'old copes' over to the still Catholic continent.

# Bibliography

The chief source for the preceding pages has been the surviving churchwardens' accounts for the period. Those which have been printed are listed below. Those in manuscript are in the Norfolk Record Office. Second in importance are the certificates and inventories of Edward VI's reign which are printed in the early volumes of *Norfolk Archaeology*.

Bond, Francis, *The Chancels of English Churches*

Brooke, Christopher, *The Medieval Church & Society*

Cardwell, E., *Documentary Annals*

Cuming, G. J., *A History of Anglican Liturgy*

Dickens, A. G., *The English Reformation*

Dickinson, J. C., *Ecclesiastical History of England, Later Middle Ages*

Frere, W. H., *Visitations and Articles and Injunctions of the period of the Reformation*

Gilchrist, James, *Anglican Church Plate*

Houlbrooke, R. A., *Church courts and people in the diocese of Norwich*, Unpublished thesis Univ. of Oxford

Houlbrooke, R. A., ed., *The Letter Book of John Parkhurst, N.R.S. Vol. XLIII*

Legge, A. G., *The Ancient Register of North Elmham*

Lestrange, J., *The Church Bells of Norfolk*

Stallard, A. D., *The Transcript of the Churchwardens' Accounts of Tilney All Saints*

Tanner, J. R., *Tudor Constitutional Documents*